G000297371

THE LITTLE BOOK OF
JOKES

THIS IS A CARLTON BOOK

Text copyright © Emap Elan Network 2001, 2004
Design copyright © Carlton Books Limited 2004

This edition published by Carlton Books Limited 2004
20 Mortimer Street
London W1T 3JW

A CIP catalogue record for this book is available from
the British Library.

ISBN 1 84442 718 8

Printed in Singapore

FHM PRESENTS...

THE LITTLE BOOK OF
JOKES

CARLTON
BOOKS

**Thanks to FHM's readers
for all their jokes**

www.fhm.com/jokes

The Ordeal of Fruit

Two men shipwrecked on an island are captured by cannibals. The chief informs them the only way to avoid becoming dinner is to undergo the 'Ordeal of Fruit'. The men accept at once, and the chief sends them into the jungle to collect 100 pieces of fruit and bring them back to him. The first man comes back with 100 grapes. The chief says that if he can shove all the grapes up his arse without giggling then he will be free. But no sooner has the first grape reached his butt than the man bursts out laughing. 'What's so funny?' the chief asks. 'Don't you realize we're going to kill you now?' 'I'm sorry,' the sailor replies. 'It's just that my friend is collecting pineapples.'

Never gamble with a chemist

This deaf mute strolls into a chemist's shop to buy a packet of condoms. Unfortunately, the mute cannot see any of his required brand on the shelves, and the chemist, unable to decipher sign language, fails to understand what the man wants.

Frustrated, the deaf mute decides to take drastic action: he unzips his trousers and drops his cock on the counter, before placing a £5 note next to it. Nodding, the chemist unzips his own trousers, performs the same manoeuvres as the mute, then picks up both notes and stuffs them in his pocket.

Exasperated, the deaf mute begins to curse the chemist with a wild gesturing of his arms. 'Sorry,' the chemist says, shrugging his shoulders. 'But if you can't afford to lose, you shouldn't gamble.'

The Amish go to town

An Amish boy and his father rode into town to visit a new shopping mall. All that they saw had them reeling in amazement, but the one thing that really caught their eye was a pair of shiny 'walls' that could slide open and close effortlessly shut again. The boy looked at his father and asked,

'What is this thing, father?'

Having never seen an elevator before, the old man responded:

'Son, I have never seen anything like this in my life. I don't know what it is.'

At that moment, a fat lady in a wheelchair rolled up

FHM

to the moving walls and pressed a button. The walls opened and the lady moved between them into a small room. The walls then closed, and the boy and his father watched in awe as a series of semi-circular numbers above the walls lit up sequentially. They continued to stare as the numbers lit in reverse order. Finally the walls opened again and a gorgeous, voluptuous blonde woman stepped out. Without taking his eyes off the young woman, the father said quietly: 'Son, go get your mother ...'

Drunk driving (i)

A man is driving happily along when he is pulled over by the police. The copper approaches him and politely asks, 'Have you been drinking, sir?'

'Why?' snorts the man. 'Is there a fat bird in my car?'

He said she'd be sorry ...

From the day of their wedding, Sarah has been
nagging her husband about his past.

'Come on, tell me,' she asks again, 'how many
women have you slept with?'

'Honey, ' he says, 'if I told you, you'd just get angry.'

'No, I promise I won't,' she begs.

'Well, If you insist. Let's see. One ... two ... three ...
four ... you ... six ... seven ...'

A fisherman's mistake

A fisherman is sorting through his catch on the edge of a lake when a man sprints up to him, obviously in some distress. 'Help me please,' he gasps. 'My wife is drowning and I can't swim.' He points out to a distant figure, splashing around pathetically 100 m from the shore. 'Please save her. I'll give you a hundred quid if you do.' Nodding, the fisherman dives into the water. In a few powerful strokes, he reached the woman, puts his arm around her, and swims back to shore. Depositing her at the feet of the man, he looks up at him.

'Okay,' he says, regaining his breath, 'where's my hundred?' The man frowns back at him. 'Look,' he says. 'When I saw her going down for the third time, I thought it was my wife. But this is my mother-in-law.' The fisherman reached into his pocket. 'Just my luck,' he says. 'How much do I owe you?'

The accommodating wife

A woman complains to her friend that her husband is losing interest in sex, and he prefers nights out with the lads to the joys of copulation. Her friend tells her that to win his love she must make more effort. She advises her to cook a slap-up meal and then send him drinking with his pals down the pub. When he returns she must be dressed in her naughtiest lingerie and look her most beautiful.

The following evening, she does exactly as instructed and is dressed to kill by the time her husband returns. When he sees her lying on the bed in all her gear, he tells her to stand up and take it all off. He then tells her to do a handstand against the bathroom mirror and open her legs. This excites the woman immensely, as her husband has never been this erotic before. She does as instructed, and then he puts his face between her legs, faces the mirror and says, 'No, no ... Maybe the lads are right. A beard wouldn't suit me.'

Mistaken diagnosis

A woman is lying in the road after being run over. The driver of the vehicle that knocked her down comes to her help. 'Are you all right, love?' he asks.

'You're just a blur,' she says. 'So my sight is clearly affected.'

Very concerned, the driver leans over the woman in order to test her eyesight. 'How many fingers have I got up?' he asks her.

'Oh shit!' she replies. 'I must be paralysed from the waist down as well.'

FHM

Booby prize

After a woman meets a man in a bar, they talk and end up leaving together. They get back to his flat, and as he's showing her around, she notices that his bedroom is completely packed with teddy bears. Hundreds of them – all arranged in size, from the smallest on the shelves along the floor, to the huge daddy bears on the very top shelf.

Surprised, the woman still decides not to mention this to him. After an intense night of passion, as they are lying there together in the afterglow, the woman rolls over and asks, smiling, 'Well, how was it?'

'Well,' says the man, frowning. 'You can have any prize from the bottom shelf.'

All fingers and thumbs

While cutting wood in his workshop, Jim the carpenter slips and manages to slice all his fingers off on his powerful electric saw. He screams and runs out of the workshop, sprinting in considerable pain to the nearest hospital. After he has been waiting half an hour, a nurse emerges.

'I'm sorry, sir,' she says, 'but without your fingers, we can't do anything except stop the bleeding. Go back and get our fingers so we can sew them back on.'

Nodding forlornly, Jim wanders out of casualty. An hour later, he returns.

'Did you recover your fingers, sir?' asks the nurse.

'No,' he replied. 'I couldn't pick them up off the floor.'

The power of drugs

Enid sat at her husband's hospital bedside, watching him slowly regain consciousness as the effects of a particularly powerful anaesthetic wore off. Slowly the man's eyes fluttered open, and, seeing his wife's anxious face looming over him, he murmured, 'You're beautiful.'

An hour later the man's eyes once again opened, and he said, 'You look nice.'

'What happened to beautiful, then?' Enid enquired.

'The drugs are wearing off,' came the frail reply.

Is that a frog in your pocket ...?

A man surveys the women in a nightclub, picks out the most attractive, and takes a seat next to her at the bar. He uses all his best lines, but gets nowhere. Finally, he reaches into his pocket, takes out a small box, and pulls a frog out of it.

'Cute,' says the woman. 'Is that a pet?'

The man smiled. 'Yes, and he's good at doing tricks too.'

'Like what?'

'He eats pussy. Come back to my place and I'll prove it to you ...'

Once in the bedroom, the girl strips off and puts

the frog between her legs. The frog doesn't move. After a couple of minutes the woman looks at the immobile frog, and finally demands, 'Well?'

The man shakes his head sorrowfully, picks up the frog, and says, 'Okay, you idiot, I'm only going to show you one more time.'

The flute player

While out on a hunting expedition, a man is climbing over a fallen tree when his shotgun goes off, hitting him straight in the groin.

Rushed to hospital, he awakes from the anaesthetic to find the surgeon has done a marvellous job repairing his damaged member. As he dresses to go home, the surgeon wanders over and hands him a business card.

'This is my brother's card. I'll make an appointment for you to see him.'

The guy is shocked. 'But it says here that he's a professional flute player,' he says. 'How can he help me?'

The doctor smiles. 'Well,' he says, 'he's going to show you where to put your fingers so you don't piss in your eye.'

He's armless

A man with no arms or legs is sunbathing on the beach. He is approached by three beautiful young women who take pity on him.

The first says to him, 'Have you ever been hugged?'

The man shakes his head, and she leans down and gives him a big hug.

The second says to him, 'Have you ever been kissed?'

He shakes his head. She kisses him.

Rather abruptly, the third girl asks, 'Have you ever been fucked?'

'No,' says the man, his eyes lighting up.

'Well, you are now. The tide's coming in.'

Knickers!

After ten loyal years working at the local factory, Nigel and Trevor were laid off, so first thing Monday morning they made their way to the DSS. When asked his occupation, Nigel said, 'I'm a panty stitcher. I sew the elastic into cotton knickers.'

The clerk looked up 'panty stitcher' and, finding it to be classed as unskilled labour, gave Nigel £100 a week benefit money.

Trevor then approached the counter and explained that he was a diesel fitter. As diesel fitting was considered to be a skilled occupation, Trevor was awarded £200 a week.

When Nigel learned how much his friend was being

given he was furious, and went storming up to the clerk, demanding to know why his mate was collecting double his own pay.

'It says on my list that diesel fitters are an intrinsic part of the skilled labour force,' explained the clerk, patiently.

'What skill?' screamed Nigel. 'I sew in the elastic, he pulls the knickers on and says, "Yup – diesel fitter!"'

A medical request

A senior lecturer at a London medical college is rather surprised one afternoon when one of his most promising students breaks through the door in a clear state of distress. Sitting the lad down, the kindly old-timer waits for him to compose himself before asking, 'What on earth is the matter?'

'I can't take it anymore, doc,' wails the distressed student. 'I need to find somewhere else to live!'

'But our student digs are the best in the land,' protests the lecturer.

'No, doctor – it's this new policy of mixed living quarters. Every night when I'm trying to study, I have to push away beautiful young nurses, who have come in drunk from a night on the town and are hungry for sex.'

'I see,' says the quack. 'So how do you think I can help?'

'Oh doc,' says the desperate young man, quietly. 'You're going to have to break my arms.'

The Legion take anyone

A captain in the Foreign Legion was transferred to a desert outpost. On his first day there he noticed a very old, seedy-looking camel tied up at the back of the barracks. He asked his sergeant what this animal was for.

The sergeant replied, 'Well, sir, we're a fair distance from anywhere, and the men have natural sexual urges, so when they do, uh, we have the camel.'

The captain thinks about this, and says, 'Well, if it's good for morale, then I suppose it's all right with me.'

After he has been at the fort for about six months, the captain became very frustrated himself. Finally he could stand it no longer and so he told his sergeant,

'Bring in the camel!'

The sarge shrugged his shoulders and led the camel into the captain's quarters. The captain then got a footstool and began to have vigorous sex with the camel. As he stepped down, satisfied, and was buttoning his pants up, he asked the sergeant, 'Is that how the enlisted men do it?'

The sergeant replied, 'Well, no sir, they usually just use it to ride to the brothel in town.'

The tell-tale fingers

'I'm baffled by your yellow penis,' the doctor told his patient. 'Does anyone else in your family have this condition?'

The concerned fellow shook his head.

'Do you handle any chemicals at work?'

'I don't work. I'm unemployed.'

Well, what do you do all day?'

'Oh, I mostly sit around watching porno movies, eating Quavers.'

Mistaken identity

Two Irishmen are walking through Calcutta when an old woman wanders past. 'Hey, Seamus,' one says. 'I think that's Mother Teresa.'

'Rubbish,' says the other.

'I'm telling you it was.'

To settle the argument, they approach the lady and ask her.

'Are you Mother Teresa?'

The old woman eyes them scornfully.

'Piss off, you perverts,' she hisses.

'Jeez,' Seamus says, watching her disappear into the crowd. 'Now we'll never know.'

Not for sale in Scotland

Two Scotsmen are walking down a country lane.

'Och, Duncan,' says Jimmy all of a sudden, 'I dinnae half need a shit.'

'Well, just go behind a bush and do it, then,' replies his mate.

So Jimmy goes behind a bush, and after a while he shouts, 'Have you got any paper?'

To which Duncan replies, 'Och, don't be such a tight bastard. Leave it.'

FHM

What a wanker

Worried about his failing eyesight, a man goes to his optician – who tells him he must stop masturbating.

'Why?' asks the man, worriedly, 'Am I going blind?'

'No, your eyesight is fine,' says the optician, 'But it upsets the other patients in the waiting room.'

Ask a stupid question ...

At 7am, a lone wife hears a key in the front door.
She wanders down, bleary eyed, to find her husband
in the kitchen – drunk, with ruffled hair and lipstick
on his collar.

'I assume,' she snarls, 'that there is a very good
reason for you to come waltzing in here at seven in
the morning?'

'There is,' he replies. 'Breakfast.'

It's all in the phrasing

An Essex girl is out driving one day when her car skids at a roundabout and hits the car in front. As she's injured, an ambulance is called and a paramedic quickly arrives. 'What's your name, love?' he asks.

'Sharon,' she replies.

Looking around, the medic sees there's a lot of blood.

'Sharon,' he asks, 'where are you bleeding from?'

'Romford,' she replies.

Drunk driving (ii)

While patrolling country lanes around his local village, a young policeman notices a car being driven erratically. With a quick burst of the siren he pulls the driver over, and sternly walks up to the car to ask the gentleman whether he's been drinking.

'Oh aye,' says the man, quite proudly. 'It's Friday, so a few of the lads and I went straight to the pub after work, and I must have had about six or seven there. Then we went to the bar next door for happy hour, and they were serving these great cocktails for a pound, so I had three or four of those. Then my cousin Mick asked for a lift home – his sister's sick, you see – so I drove him back. Of course, he asked me in, so I had a

Murphy's – lovely stuff it is, too – and took a bottle for the road.'

With that, the man reaches into his coat, pulls out a bottle of scotch, waves it at the policeman, and beams happily.

'Sir, would you exit the vehicle immediately for a breathalyser test,' the officer says as calmly as he can.

'Why?' asks the man. 'Don't you believe me?'

Twin controls

Two Siamese twins go on holiday to the same resort in southern France every year. Unsurprisingly, the head waiter recognizes the conjoined brothers, and asks if they keep coming back for the weather.

'Oh no,' replies one of the twins, 'Actually we burn quite easily.'

'Perhaps you are wine connoisseurs, then?' wonders the waiter.

'Again, no,' says the other twin. 'We're both beer drinkers'

'I know!' cries the waiter. 'It must be the fine French food?'

'Actually,' they say, shaking their heads, 'We prefer

English fish and chips.'

The waiter is astounded. 'So what makes you come back year after year?'

'Well,' says one twin, pointing to his brother. 'It's the only chance our kid gets to drive.'

Caught short

A girl takes her new boyfriend back home after the dance. She tells him to be very, very quiet as her parents are asleep upstairs and if they wake up, she would be in big trouble as she's not allowed to bring boys home.

They settle down to business on the sofa, but after a while, he stops and says, 'Where's the toilet, I need to go.'

She says, 'It's next to my parents' bedroom. You can't go there, you might wake them up. Use the sink in the kitchen instead.'

He goes into the kitchen then, after a short while, he pops his head round the door and says to his girlfriend, 'Have you got any paper?'

Sand trap

Pinocchio complains to his father saying 'Whenever I attempt to make love to a woman, she complains of splinters.' His father shows pity and gives Pinocchio a piece of sandpaper to smooth his knob down whenever he needs to. A few days later during dinner his father asks, 'How are the girls?' Pinocchio replies, 'Girls? Who needs girls?'

Chinese takeaway

A man goes to a disco and starts chatting up a very attractive-looking Chinese girl. After a night of cavorting, she asks him back to her place 'for a coffee'. They get to her flat, and she tells him to help himself to a drink while she slips into something more comfortable. Just as he finishes his drink, the sexy Chinese seductress returns wearing only a see-through negligée.

'I am your sex slave!' she says. 'I will do absolutely ANYTHING you want.'

The man can't believe his luck. 'Hmm,' he says, grinning from ear-to-ear.

'I really fancy a 69.'

'Fuck off!' replies the girl. 'I'm not cooking at this time of night.'

Shhh!

A blonde walks into a library.

'Excuse me – can I have a burger and large fries, please?' she demands.

Tutting, the librarian looks back at her. 'Miss,' he says, 'this is a library.'

The blonde leans over the counter.

'I'm sorry,' she whispers. 'Can I have a burger and large fries, please?'

The interpretation of dreams

Waking after a long night's sleep, a wife begins recounting her dream to her husband. 'I dreamt I was at an auction for cocks,' she began. 'The long ones went for a tenner, and the meaty ones for £20.'

'How about the ones like mine?' asked her husband.

'Oh, they gave those away,' she replied, grinning slyly.

Miffed, the husband responds: 'Well I had a dream too – where they were auctioning off pussies. The pretty ones cost £1,000 and the little tight ones went for double that.'

'And how much for the ones like mine?' inquired his wife. The man grinned. 'Oh, that's where they held the auction.'

Lucky Dog

Three guys are comparing their drunkenness from the night before. The first guy says, 'I was so drunk I don't even know how I got home ... I just woke up in my bed in a pool of sweat.'

'Oh yeah?' brags the second guy. 'I was so wasted I took home a strange woman and was having sex with her when my wife walked in.'

'That's nothing,' says the third guy. 'I was so pissed I was blowing Chunks all night.'

'Big deal,' scoff the other two.

The third guy says, 'I don't think you understand – Chunks is the name of my dog.'

At least someone's happy

A doctor walks into his office, where a patient is anxiously awaiting results from a blood test. 'Mr Stirling, I'm not going to mess you around,' the medic announces. 'There's good news and bad news. Which do you want?'

'Give me the bad stuff,' replies the man.

Calmly, the doc says, 'You've got 48 hours to live.'

His patient howls, claws his hair and moans, 'Oh my God, what am I going to do? Surely there must be a cure!'

'Of course not,' says the doctor, gruffly.

'But I thought you said there was some good news,' sobs the man.

FHM

'Oh yes, that's right – there is,' replies the quack, cheerfully. 'Remember the beautiful nurse at reception when you came in?'

'Yes,' replies the puzzled patient.

'The blonde with the tight, white uniform?'

'Yeah! With the big tits!' says the patient, brightening up somewhat.

'Well,' says the doctor, leaning over to whisper. 'I'm shagging her.'

Dispute down under

The Australian Prime Minister flies to England for a meeting with the Queen. Over a cup of tea, the PM brings up his grand new plan for his country.

'Your Majesty, mate,' he begins. 'Can we turn Australia into a kingdom, in order to increase our role in the global economy?'

The Queen shakes her head and replies, 'One needs a king for a kingdom, and unfortunately you are most certainly not a king.'

Not to be dissuaded, the politician asks, 'Would it be possible to transform Australia into an empire, then?'

'No,' replies the Queen. 'For an empire you need an

FHM

emperor, and you are most certainly not an emperor.' The PM thinks for a moment and then asks if it's possible to turn Australia into a principality.

The Queen replies, 'For a principality, you need a prince – and you are not a prince.' Pausing for a sip of her tea, Her Majesty then adds: 'I don't mean to appear rude, but having met both you and several other Australians, I think Australia is perfectly suited as a country.'

Transfer of guilt

Liverpool Football Club are on the look out for some new talent and send a scout to Bosnia where they find a fantastic new player and bring him back with them. In his first game, he scores a hat-trick and the fans love him. When he gets home he decides to phone his mum and give her the good news, but when she answers she immediately starts crying.

When he asks what the matter is, she replies, 'Well, this morning your sister was raped by a street gang, then your little brother was savaged by wild dogs while playing football in the street. After that your dad was shot by a sniper and I was mugged and beaten up while shopping.'

The guy is gobsmacked. 'Mum, what can I say? I'm so sorry.'

'Sorry?!' she shouts. 'It's your fault we moved to Liverpool!'

Countdown

After months of ill-health, a man goes to his doctor for a complete check-up. Afterward, the doctor comes out with the results.

'I'm afraid I have some very bad news,' says the physician. 'You're dying, and you don't have much time left.'

'Oh, that's terrible!' says the man. 'How long have I got?'

'Ten,' the doctor replies, shaking his head.

'Ten?' the man asks. 'Ten what? Months? Weeks? What do you mean?'

The doctor looks at him sadly. 'Nine ...'

FHM

Marital economics

Little Johnny walks past his parents room one night and sees them making love. Puzzled, he asks his father about it in the morning. 'Why were you doing that to mummy last night?'

His father replies, 'Because mummy wants a baby.'

The next night, Johnny spots mummy giving daddy a blow job and the next morning he asks his father, 'Why was mummy doing that to you last night?'

His father replies, 'Because mummy wants a BMW.'

Dearth of a princess

Princess Diana and the Queen are being driven around the grounds of Balmoral, when the Land Rover is stopped by a robber. He tells the Queen to wind down her window and hand over all her money.

'I'm the richest woman in the world,' replies the Queen. 'I have no need for money.'

So the robber turns to Diana and demands she hands over all her jewellery.

'I'm the most beautiful woman in the world,' replies Di. 'I have no need for jewellery.'

The robber decides to cut his losses and so steals the Land Rover instead. When he's gone, the Queen asks Diana where she hid all her jewellery.

FHM

'Well,' says Diana, 'when I saw him approaching, I stuffed it all up my fanny. Why, what did you do with all the money you were carrying?'

'Same thing,' says the Queen. 'When I saw him approaching, I stuffed all the cash up my fanny.'

'It's a pity Fergie wasn't here,' says Diana. 'Otherwise we could have saved the Land Rover as well.'

Size does matter

Three men are marooned on a desert island desperately seeking a way to get off. A cannibal approaches them and flops his penis out. 'If the length of your three penises put together is as big as mine, then I'll show you a way to get off the island,' he says. 'But otherwise you'll be killed and eaten.'

The native's love muscle was a staggering 20 inches. The first man got his out, and it was 10 inches. The second man then produced a 9-inch knob. Realizing they only needed 1 inch to go, the first two men were quietly confident. The third got his penis out, and it was only 1 inch long.

After some tense calculations, the native says,

'Okay, you've equalled the length of my penis. I have a boat which you can use to escape.'

While sailing away on the boat, the first man says to the other two, 'You're lucky I've got a 10-inch penis.'

And the second says, 'You're lucky I've got a 9-inch penis.'

To which the third man replies, 'And you're lucky I had an erection.'

Happy meal

One cold winter evening, an elderly couple wander into a fast-food restaurant. As the young families look on, the old gent walks up to the counter, orders a meal and then pays. Taking a seat next to his wife, he slowly unwraps the plain burger and cuts it in two – placing one half in front of his beloved. Then, he carefully divides the fries into two piles: one for him, one for her.

As the man takes a few bites of hamburger, the crowd began to get restless – this is obviously a couple who've been together for decades, and all they can afford is a single meal. Eventually, a young onlooker wanders over and offers to buy another meal.

'We're just fine, thanks,' says the pensioner. 'After 50 years, we're used to sharing everything.'

Then the young man notices that the little old lady hasn't eaten a bite of her portion. Instead, while her husband wolfs down his half, she sits and occasionally sips the drink.

'Ma'am,' says the young chap. 'Why aren't you eating? Your husband says you share everything. What are you waiting for?'

Over horn-rimmed glasses, she looks back at him. 'The teeth,' she says.

Two countries separated by a common language

A tourist walks into a drug store in Los Angeles, and asks for a packet of condoms. 'Rubbers, eh?' says the chemist, recognizing his customer is English. 'That'll be five dollars – including the tax.'

'Is that necessary?' cries the man. 'Back home, we roll them on.'

FHM

The taxman cometh

A Yuletide meal at an expensive restaurant is disturbed when a woman starts screaming. 'My son's choking! ' she cries. 'He's swallowed the sixpence in the Christmas pudding! Please, anyone – help!'

Without speaking, a man stands up at a nearby table, and walks over nonchalantly. Smiling pleasantly, he grips the boy by the gonads and squeezes: the boy coughs, and out pops the coin.

'Thank you so much!' beams the relieved mother. 'Are you a paramedic?'

'No,' replied the man, 'I work for the Inland Revenue.'

Builder's arse

One day a construction crew arrives next door to a young family to build another house. The family's six-year-old daughter naturally takes an interest, and begins hanging around the site. Eventually the brickies adopt her as a kind of mascot – chatting to her and giving her errands to run. Then, at the end of the week, they present her with a pay envelope containing a fiver.

Excitedly, the little girl runs home to her mother, who suggests they take it to the bank. Running straight up to the pay-in desk, the little girl thrusts her wages over the counter.

'I earned this building a house,' she beams, proudly.

'For a whole week.'

'Goodness!' smiles the teller. 'And will you be building it next week, too?'

'Yes,' trills the little girl. 'If the fucking bricks ever get delivered.'

Calling all cars ...

A burglary was recently committed at Manchester City's ground and the entire contents of the trophy room were stolen. Police are looking for a man with a pale blue carpet.

Know your own strength

Sven-Goran Eriksson arrives for his first training session as England manager, and wanders into the changing room – only to spot a massive, steaming turd nestling in the middle of the shower room. Fuming, he returns to his players in the main changing area.

'Who's shit on the floor?' he screams.

'Me, boss,' cries Emile Heskey, 'but I'm not bad in the air.'

Can I get some privacy?

Little Red Riding Hood is walking through the woods one day, when she spies the wolf crouched down behind a bush. Thinking that it would be a laugh and make a bit of a change to sneak up on him for once, she creeps over and taps the wolf on his shoulder.

'My, mister wolf,' she says with a smirk, 'what big eyes you have. Don't you want to play?'

'Leave me alone!' the wolf cries, and runs off. Riding Hood trails him for a way, and finds him behind an old oak tree.

'My, mister wolf,' she says, 'what big ears you have. Don't you want to play?'

'For God's sake, please leave me alone!' the beast

66

howls, and runs off into the woods. Riding Hood strikes out after him, and discovers him in a patch of old stinging nettles.

'My, mister wolf,' she says, 'what big teeth you have. Don't you want to play?'

'For Christ's sake, leave me alone!' the wolf barks in fury. 'I'm trying to have a shit!'

The awkward customer

Cursed with a bald head and a wooden leg, a man is
surprised to learn that he's been invited to a fancy
dress party. Deciding that he might pull it off if he
wears a costume to hide his head and leg, he writes to
a theatrical outfitters asking them for advice. A few
days later, he receives a parcel from the company with
a note that says, 'Dear Sir. Please find enclosed a
pirate's outfit. The spotted handkerchief will cover your
bald head, and with your wooden leg you will be just
right as a buccaneer.'

Unfortunately, the man finds this deeply insulting, as
they have so clearly emphasized his wooden leg, so he
fires off a letter of complaint. A week passes before

the postman delivers another parcel with a note that reads, 'Dear Sir, sorry about our previous suggestion – please find enclosed a monk's habit. The long robe will cover your wooden leg and with your bald head you will really look the part.'

This infuriates the man again, because they have simply switched from emphasizing his wooden leg to his balding head, so he writes the company another letter of complaint. The next day he receives a tiny parcel and a hastily scrawled note, which reads:

'Dear Sir, please find enclosed a tin of treacle. Pour it over your head, stick your wooden leg up your arse and go as a toffee apple, you grumpy twat.'

Justice, South African style

Three men in a prison in South Africa; two white, one black. The first white guy says, 'I'm in for six years for robbery. The judge said I was lucky. If it had been armed robbery, I would have got ten.'

The second white man says, 'I'm in for 15 years for manslaughter. The judge said I was lucky. If it had been first degree murder, I would have got more than 20.'

The black man says, 'I got 20 years for riding without my bicycle lights on. The judge says I was lucky. If it had been dark at the time, he would have given me life.'

FHM

The numbers game

A man is strolling past a lunatic asylum when he hears a loud chanting. 'Thirteen! Thirteen! Thirteen!' goes the noise from within the mental hospital's wards.

The man's curiosity gets the better of him and he searches for a hole in the security fence. It's not long before he finds a small crack, so he leans forward and peers in. Instantly, someone jabs him in the eye.

As he reels back in agony, the chanting continues: 'Fourteen! Fourteen! Fourteen!'

Holiday dilemma

The Good Lord is up in Heaven, moaning about the pressures and stresses of omnipotence and being Number One. He decides it's time to go on holiday.

He summons all his superbeing mates and they pop round with a few suggestions. 'What about Mars?' says one.

'Nah,' replies God. 'I went there 15,000 years ago, and it was awful – no atmosphere and too dusty.'

'Pluto?' suggests another.

'No way,' God pipes up. 'I went there 10,000 years ago. Freezing. Awful place.'

'Well,' says another of God's protégés. 'How about Mercury?'

God turns the suggestion down. 'Been there. Nearly burnt my nuts off – never again.'

'Okay,' says another of God's favourite cronies. 'How about Earth?'

'Woah!' God exclaims. 'Not a chance! I went there about 2,000 years ago, knocked up some bird and they're still bloody talking about it!'

Load of balls

While holidaying in southern Spain a man visits a local restaurant – where he sees a diner happily wolfing down two large pink objects. 'I'll have those, please,' he tells the waiter.

'I'm sorry, Senor,' comes the reply, 'but they are cojones – the testicles of the bull killed in the local bullfight. We won't have any more until after the next fight.'

Disappointed, the man returns after the next fight. The waiter remembers him and brings out a plate of two steaming balls. 'Just a minute,' says the man. 'These are tiny. The ones the man had were four times as big.'

The waiter shrugs. 'Senor – sometimes the bull, he win.'

FHM

Short tempered

The supervisor of a local firm is somewhat startled when his secretary bursts into his office and demands to file a complaint of sexual harassment against a man who works in the same department.

'What on earth did he do?' asks the concerned boss.

'It's not what he did, it's what he said!' she shrieks. 'He said that my hair smelt nice!'

'And what's so wrong with telling you that?' asks the supervisor, confused.

'He's a midget,' huffs the woman.

Good dog!

There were three rottweilers in the waiting room at the vet's surgery, and after a while they got talking.

'I was out walking with my master,' says the first one, 'when a thug attacked him, so I chased the guy, caught him by the throat and savaged him to death. That's why I'm here to be put down.'

'I was in the house,' began the second dog, 'when a burglar broke in and tried to nick the TV. So I pinned him to the floor, bit his arm off, and now I'm here to be put down.'

The third rottweiler then started his story. 'I was patrolling the house one evening, and I wandered into

FHM

the bathroom to see my master's wife naked, bending over the tub, so I leapt up and gave her a good seeing-to from behind.'

'What, and you're being put down for that?'

'Oh, no. I'm just here to get my claws clipped.'

Going bats

Two bats are out searching for a midnight feed. After a while they reunite at the belfry. Boris is still starving, not having found a thing to eat. But Brian comes in licking his lips, fresh blood oozing from his mouth and fangs.

'Wow,' exclaims Boris. 'I couldn't even find a mouse to eat. Where on earth did you get all that from?'

'Come on, I'll show you,' replies Brian, and off they venture into the night. After a few moments, Brian slows to a hover and whispers, 'Right. See that tree?'

'Uh-huh,' murmurs Boris.

'I didn't,' says Brian.

FHM

Right-winger

After a heavy night in his local pub, a worse-for-wear lout rises to his feet, determined to start up a fight.

'Right,' he hollers, 'everybody on the left side of the pub is a bastard!'

The drinkers look across at him briefly, then resume their drinking.

'No takers, eh?' shouts the piss-head. 'Right then – everyone on the right side is a poofter!'

Suddenly, an old man on the left-hand side of the pub stands up. 'You want some, then?' screams the lout.

'Not really,' replies the man, sheepishly. 'It's just that I appear to be sitting on the wrong side of the pub.'

FHM

Loaded for bear

An extremely wealthy 80-year-old man arrived for his annual check-up and smiled when the doctor enquired about his health.

'Never better,' he announced proudly. 'I've taken an 18-year-old bride, and she's pregnant. What do you think of that?'

The doctor considered this for a moment, then said, 'I once knew a guy who was an avid hunter. One day he slept late and in the subsequent rush, he dashed out with his umbrella instead of his rifle.'

'Go on, doc,' says the old-timer.

'Deep in the woods, he faced a huge, angry bear, raised his umbrella, pointed it at the animal and

FHM

squeezed the handle. And do you know what happened?'

Dumbfounded, the old codger shook his head.

'The bear fell dead in front of him.'

'That's impossible,' exclaimed the old man. 'Someone else must have been doing the shooting.'

Sighing, the doctor gave his patient a friendly pat on the back.

'That's what I'm getting at.'

Farmer in the dock

A well-known farmer is caught in a mindless act of bestiality with an ox on his farm, and – after much public humiliation and ridicule from the police – looks up both the village lawyers. He finds himself faced with two choices. The first lawyer has a brilliant reputation of finding a sympathetic jury, but has a history of making ludicrous statements and summing up in a disastrous fashion. The second is a fantastic debater and a real case-winner, but is always plagued by juries that want to lynch him. The farmer eventually settles on the first one.

A week later, sitting in court, his lawyer stands, adjusts his tie and turns to the jury. 'My client,' he says confidently, 'approached the ox from behind, took it by surprise, grabbed it hard by its flanks, and went at it hell for leather. When he had finished, he casually walked round to the front of the beast, who proceeded to lick his penis clean.'

The farmer stares at his lawyer in disbelief, cursing himself for hiring such an obvious simpleton, when suddenly the jury nod enthusiastically and the foreman whispers, 'Mmm, yes – a good ox will do that.'

What do you expect from a horse?

Roy Rogers is riding through the Wild West on his trusty horse, Trigger, when he happens upon Apache Indians. Not best pleased at having trespassers in their territory, the Indians capture Roy and bury him up to his chin in the sand. Before leaving him to die in the scorching heat, the Indians grant him one last wish. 'Could I say a parting farewell to my trusty steed?' comes the request. The Indians seem to understand, and agree, so Roy beckons Trigger to come closer then whispers in his ear. The horse bolts off at once in the direction of the nearest town.

Half an hour later, the horse returns bearing a scantily clad, gorgeous prostitute. The prostitute jumps

down off the horse and gently removes the small, frilly knickers she's wearing. Sitting astride Roy Rogers' face, she proceeds to give him firsts, seconds and thirds of her fanny, almost suffocating him in the process.

Well, the Indians think this is magic and decide that he deserves another wish. So Roy beckons his horse again and whispers in his ear.

'I said fetch a posse, you stupid git!'

Love me, love my dog

Feeling very depressed, a man walks into a pub and orders a triple scotch. 'You know,' says the barman, pouring him the drink. 'That's quite a heavy poison. Is something wrong?'

'Well,' says the man, downing the shots in one. 'I got home and found my wife in bed with my best friend.'

'Wow!' exclaims the bartender. 'No wonder you need a drink – this one's on the house. What did you do?'

'I walked over to my wife', the man replies, 'and told her that we were through. I told her to get the hell out.'

'That makes sense', says the bartender, nodding. 'But what about your best friend?'

'Well,' slurs the man, tears in his eyes. 'I walked over to him, looked him right in the eye, and said "Bad dog!"'

FHM

Mistaken identity

Feeling rather daring, a grey-haired old woman goes to a tattoo parlour. 'I want a picture of Frank Bruno on my left inner thigh and a picture of Mike Tyson on my right inner thigh,' she says to the tattooist.

When he's finished, she looks at her new tattoos. Disgusted, she says, 'These are rubbish! I want to see the manager.'

The manager comes out, 'What seems to be the problem, madam?' he asks.

'I wanted a tattoo of Frank Bruno and Mike Tyson and they don't look like either of them!'

The manager steps back to take a look. 'You're right, they don't. But the one in the middle is definitely Don King.'

Are you local?

Hopelessly lost, a businessman approaches a local in a village.

'Excuse me,' he says, 'but what's the quickest way to York?'

The local scratches his head. 'Are you walking or driving?' he asks.

'I'm driving,' comes the reply.

'Hmm,' mulls the local. 'I'd say that's definitely the quickest way.'

Sticky wicket

The Lone Ranger and his faithful chum, Tonto, are riding down a hillside in the Wild West, when Tonto suddenly stops, gets off his horse and puts his head to the ground.

'Buffalo come,' Tonto said.

'Amazing! How do you know?' asks the Lone Ranger.

'Ear stuck to ground,' replies Tonto.

Sweet chastity

A brave knight has to go off to fight in the Crusades and leaves his sexy wife at home. As he can't trust his wife to be left on her own, he fits her with a very special chastity belt made out of razor blades. On his victorious return, he lines up all his male staff, and makes them drop their trousers. He is greeted by a whole line of shredded todgers, apart from one. He goes up to that man and said, 'I trusted you and, unlike all the others, you have not betrayed my trust. In return I shall give you half my land.'

To which the man replies, 'Ugg ou gery muk.'

FHM

Moo!

Two cows in a field. One says to the other,

'What do you make of this mad cow disease?'

The other one says, 'Doesn't affect me, mate.'

'Oh, yeah? Why's that?'

'I'm a helicopter.'

Smells funny

After years of flirting, a man and woman in an old people's home agree to make love – and one day, when the residents go on a day trip, they both stay behind. Impatient for his first action in decades, the man quickly goes to the woman's room and asks her if there's anything she prefers. She replies she loves it when men perform cunnilingus on her – and grinning widely, the man goes down.

After a few seconds, however, he reappears. 'I'm sorry,' he says, 'but I'm afraid the smell is just too bad.'

'Hmmm,' she replies, thinking for a moment. 'It must be the arthritis.'

He looks at her confused. 'Surely you can't get

arthritis down there,' he cries, 'And even if you could, it wouldn't cause that smell.'

'No, the arthritis is in my shoulder,' she bleats. 'I can't wipe my arse.'

Surprise package

At the end of the primary school term, a kindergarten teacher is receiving gifts from her departing pupils. First up is the local florist's son, whose gift is a well-wrapped cone. 'I bet I know what it is,' she says, after shaking it and inhaling deeply. 'Have you got me flowers?'

'That's right!' cries the boy. 'But how did you know?'

'Just a wild guess,' she said, grinning.

The next pupil was the daughter of the local sweetshop owner. Again, the teacher held her box over her head, shook it, and heard the soft rattle.

'Thank you,' she says, 'I love chocolates!'

'That's right! But how did you know?' asked the girl.

'Just a lucky guess,' laughs the teacher.

Finally, the son of the local off-licence owner shyly approaches. Again, the teacher holds his box above her head and shakes it side to side – only to find it leaking.

'Mmmm,' she says, tasting a drop of the leakage with her finger. 'Is it wine?'

Open-mouthed, the youngster shakes his head – and the teacher repeats the process. 'Oh. Is it a nice vintage champagne, perhaps?' she asks.

Again, the boy shakes his head excitedly.

'OK,' admits the teacher, 'I give up. What is it?'

The boy laughs in delight. 'A puppy!'

Desert island dicks

A man who has been shipwrecked on a desert island for several years is beginning to feel the effects of being starved of sex for so long. However, the only living creatures on the island are a pig and a dog. One day, the man decides he's had enough and thinks to himself that it has to be the pig. But when he approaches the sow for his moment of passion, the dog bites the man's backside. This continues for several days, and the man is beginning to get very frustrated.

But one morning, the man's luck changes: out to sea, he notices a beautiful young woman on the point of drowning. He swims over, drags her out on to the beach and proceeds to give her the kiss of life. The woman comes to and is very grateful.

'Thank you so much,' she says. 'I will do anything for you, and I mean absolutely anything.'

The man can't believe his luck and quickly replies, 'You wouldn't mind taking that bloody dog for a walk, would you?'

The mumbling midget

One morning, a stud farm owner receives a visit from a midget wanting to buy a horse. It soon becomes obvious that the dwarf has a bad speech impediment. 'Can I view a female horth?' he asks.

Dutifully, the owner leads one out, and shows the midget the hoofs and legs. 'That'th a thtrong looking beatth, for thure,' says the gnomic breeder, nodding his head. 'Can I thee her mouf?'

Confused as to how the tiny man will ride the animal, the farmer still picks up the midget by his braces and shows him the horse's mouth.

'Nith, healthy-looking horth,' agrees the midget. 'Now move me awownd to her eerth ...'

Now getting annoyed, the owner lifts up the midget one more time to look at the ears.

'Finally,' says the Lilliputian, 'can I see her twat?'

With that, the owner picks up the midget and shoves his head into the horse's vagina. He pulls him out after a minute, and the tiny man stumbles around, dazed.

'Perhapth I thould rephrathe that,' says the midget, shaking his head. 'Can I thee her wun awownd?'

Never satisfied

Two rabbits, who have spent their whole lives in a laboratory, are set free one night by an animal activist. They run off into the countryside and come across a field of carrots. Instinct takes over: they get stuck in and start to eat all the carrots they can, until they fall asleep.

The following night, they go into a field of cabbages. Again, they eat all they can and fall asleep. The night after that, they find a field full of lettuce, which, as before, they proceed to chomp through until they fall asleep.

The next night they find themselves in a field full of lady rabbits, all of whom are willing partners. They do

FHM

what comes naturally and embark upon an all-night shagging session. In the morning, the older rabbit decides he wants to return to the lab.

'What the hell for?' asks his pal. 'We've had carrots, cabbages, lettuce and, best of all, those ladies last night. What's your problem?'

'Life is sweet, I agree,' says the older chap. 'But the thing is, I'm dying for a fag!'

Earning her money

Knowing that he'll be back late from work, Joe asks his workmate Barry to pop by his house to let his wife know what time he'll be home. Barry agrees and sets off. Joe's wife opens the door and invites Barry in, as she's just finishing her ironing. Barry passes on his news and notices that Joe's wife is ironing her underwear.

'I tell you what,' says Barry. 'I know you're a bit hard up at the moment, so if you dance around for me in that underwear, I'll give you £40.'

Needing the money, she reluctantly agrees. After the dance, Barry continues, 'Now I'll make it £100 if you do that naked.' A little sheepishly, she strips off her

undies and repeats the dance.

'Now,' says an excited Barry, 'I'll make it £200 if you let me give you one.' Feeling ashamed but desperate for the money, she again agrees. When Barry finishes, he thanks her, pays her the money and leaves. Thirty minutes later, Joe returns from work to find his wife watching the telly.

'All right, love? Did Barry tell you I'd be late?' Still embarrassed, she nods.

'Oh, and love,' Joe goes on, 'did he give you my wages?'

The fearless firemen

During a particularly dry summer, a chemical plant bursts into flames, and the alarm goes out to all available fire departments. Twenty engines duly arrive, and spend the next three hours battling the inferno. Eventually, with little sign of the fire being put out, the company director runs over and says: 'All of our industrial secrets are still in there. I'll offer £50,000 to any team that can salvage them.'

With renewed vigour, the firemen try to quench the flames, but to no avail. Suddenly, a dilapidated old engine with a volunteer crew of geriatrics comes screaming down the street, straight into the middle of the inferno. The other firefighters can only watch in

awe as the old fellas hop out and bring the flames under control in ten minutes.

As he writes out the cheque, the company director says to the chief fireman: 'You old boys have done a great job. But tell me, what will you do with the money?'

The smoke-addled elderly gent peers at him, coughs, and says:

'Well, the first thing is to get some fucking brakes for that truck.'

Be gentle with me

A bloke walks into the doctor's surgery looking very sheepish. The doctor asks him what the problem is and he explains that it's a rather delicate matter to do with his back passage, which he finds a bit difficult to talk about.

The doctor says, 'Look, I've been in this profession for 26 years and there isn't much I haven't seen. I understand you're embarrassed about it, but it would save us both a lot of time if you just told me.'

'I think I'd find it a lot easier if I just showed you,' the man replied. The doctor agrees, so the man drops his trousers and bends over. The sight of the guy's arsehole renders the doctor speechless; it has been torn to the size of a football and is badly bruised.

'Jesus Christ!' said the doctor, 'What the hell happened to you?'

'Well,' the bloke says, 'I was on Safari in Kenya and I got raped by a bull elephant.'

The doctor considers this for a second and says, 'Well, with my rather limited knowledge of veterinary science, I thought elephants' penises were very long and very thin.'

'That's right, doctor,' the guy agrees, 'but he fingered me first.'

Bringing them round

Two young guys are picked up by the cops for smoking dope and appear in court before the judge. The judge tells them, 'You seem like nice young men, and I'd like to give you a second chance rather than jail time. I want you to go out this weekend and show others the evils of drug use and get them to give up drugs forever. I'll see you back in court on Monday.'

When the two guys return to court, the judge asks the first one, 'So, how did you do over the weekend?'

'Well, your Honour, I managed to persuade 17 people to give up drugs forever.'

'Seventeen people? That's wonderful. What did you tell them?'

FHM

'I used a diagram, your Honour. I drew two circles like this – O o – and explained to them that the big circle is your brain before drugs and that the small circle is your brain after drugs.'

'That's admirable,' said the judge, turning to the second guy. 'And you, how did you do?'

'Well, Your Honour, I managed to persuade 156 people to give up drugs forever.'

'156 people! That's amazing! How did you manage to do that!'

'Well, I used the same diagram, only I pointed to the small circle first and said this is your arsehole before prison ...'

In the bakers

A Glaswegian walks into a bakers, and looks at the array of cakes on offer. 'Scuse me,' he barks at the assistant, in his thick Scottish brogue. 'But is that a macaroon, or a meringue?'

'No, you're right,' says the woman behind the counter. 'It is a macaroon.'

The city of love

A young Australian is enjoying his first night in Rome. He's drinking cappuccino at a pavement cafe when a pretty girl sat herself beside him. 'Hello,' he says, 'do you understand English?'

'Only a little,' she replies.

'How much?' he asks.

'Fifty dollars,' she replies.

Sex education

Young Judith runs out to the backyard, where her father is chopping wood. She looks up at the hardworking parent, smiles, and asks: 'Daddy, what is 'sex'?'

Laying down his axe, the old-timer sits beside his daughter and starts to explain about the birds and the bees. Then he tells her about conception, sperm and eggs. Next he thinks, 'What the hell – I might as well explain the whole works,' and goes into great detail about puberty, menstruation, erections and wet dreams. Judith's eyes bulge as her old man continues his lesson, moving on to masturbation, oral, anal and group sex, pornography, bestiality, dildos and homosexuality.

Realizing he has probably gone too far, the father pauses and asks,

'So, Judith, why do you want to know about sex?'

'Well,' says the fresh-faced youngster. 'Mummy said to tell you that lunch will be ready in a couple of secs.'

Slip of the tongue

A guy is talking to his friend and says, 'Man, I made the most embarrassing mistake yesterday. I went to the airport and the woman behind the counter had these beautiful big breasts, and I asked her for two pickets to Tittsburgh!'

'Yeah, I know what you mean,' his friend replied. 'Just this morning I meant to ask my wife to pass the salt and I said 'BITCH, YOU RUINED MY LIFE!"

Fleas take a break

Two fleas are planning a holiday at the other end of
the house. One flea turns to the other and says:
'Should we hop or take the cat?'

For you, the war is over

At the start of World War One, a father approaches his son to explain he has to go to fight for his country. Nodding, his son asks that on his return could he bring back a souvenir from the battlefields – perhaps a German helmet. 'You know,' says the boy, 'One with a spike on top.'

And so, weeks later the man is out on the mud-soaked fields of Flanders, when he spies a German helmet lying in the mud. Bending down to pick it up, he finds it stuck fast; as he grasps the spike for a better grip, he realizes there is a German soldier still attached underneath.

'If you pull me out of ze dirt, you can tek me

prisoner,' says the soldier, through the grime.

'If I pull you out,' says the Brit, 'can I have your helmet for my son?'

'Ja – be my guest!' comes the German's cheerful reply.

And so, with great effort, he begins to pull the soldier from the ground. But, after half an hour, he's still only managed to get him up to his waist.

'I'm bloody knackered,' he says, catching his breath.

'Vud it help,' replies the German soldier, 'Iff I took my feet out of ze stirrups?'

Good reception

A woman rushes into the foyer of a large hotel and sprints up to the reception desk. Seeing that the only member of staff is talking on the phone, she hammers on the bell for service.

The receptionist slowly puts down the phone. 'Yes?' he says, wearily.

'Excuse me,' says the woman, 'But I'm in a frightful hurry. Could you check me out, please?'

The clerk stares at her for a second and looks her up and down.

'Not bad,' he smiles. 'Not bad at all.'

FHM

Drunk driving (iii)

While walking his beat, a policeman is bemused to find a young man, clearly drunk, staggering about with a key in his hand.

'They've stolen my car,' the drunk shouts. 'It was right here earlier on the end of this key.'

'More importantly, sir,' says the policeman. 'Do you know your penis is hanging out?'

'Oh my God,' wails the drunk. 'They've got my girlfriend as well.'

Lucky motorist

On holiday in Ireland, an American is happily driving through Donegal in the Cadillac he has shipped over from home. But on the third day, his car breaks down, leaving him stranded in the country. He opens the hood but just stands there, staring, not knowing how to fix it.

Then from nowhere he hears a voice saying: 'Check the battery connections.' He turns around but there is no one there. He checks the battery connections and finds them loose, so tightens them up; the car starts and he drives off.

A couple of yards down the road he spots a nice pub and goes in for lunch. He ends up chatting to the barman and tells him of the incident.

'Ah, you must have been at O'Conner's farm,' says the barman.

'I was near a farm – but how do you know it was O'Conner's?' asks the Yank.

'Was there a little bridge?'

'Yes, there was' the man replies.

'And to your left was there a grey mare and a black stallion in the bottom field?' the barman probes.

'Gee, there was,' the holidaymaker retorts.

'Ahh, you're a lucky man,' laughs the publican. 'The grey mare knows nothing about engines.'

Getting the hump

Quasimodo asks Esmerelda one day if he really is the ugliest man alive. Esmerelda says, 'Go upstairs and ask the magic mirror who is the ugliest man alive and the magic mirror will tell you.'

Five minutes later, Quasimodo comes back and sits down.

After a while, Esmerelda says, 'Well?'

To which Quasimodo says, 'Who's Iain Dowie?'

Wrong number

A rich man is away on a business trip and phones home. The maid answers and he asks if he can speak to his wife.

'She's upstairs having sex with her lover,' the undiplomatic home-help replies.

'Right,' says the man, 'go upstairs. Take out my shotgun and shoot them both.'

The maid leaves, and the man hears two loud shots, then the maid returns. 'What shall I do with the bodies?' she asks.

'Take them out the back,' the man says. 'And dump them in the swimming pool.'

'What swimming pool?' the maid asks.

'That is 849 9698, isn't it?' asks the man.

Ye Gods!

Thor, the Viking God of Thunder, and Odin, the King of the Gods, are enjoying a flagon of mead in Valhalla, the Norse heaven. Suddenly, Thor turns to Odin.

'You know, my Lord,' he says, thoughtfully thumbing his mystical hammer. 'Being a god is brilliant, but it's been millennia since I had any sex.'

Odin nodded and pondered for a while. Raising his mighty head, he took pity on his subordinate.

'Go to Earth, Thor,' he replied. 'Find thyself there what they call a "lady of the night". Treat her to your manly pleasures.'

Bowing gracefully, Thor retired and followed Odin's advice, before returning the next night.

FHM

'My Lord,' he said, grinning from ear to ear, 'You were right – it was wonderful. We had passionate sex 37 times!'

'Thirty-seven times?' exclaimed Odin. 'That poor woman! Mere mortals cannot endure such treatment. You must go and apologize this instant!'

Humbled, Thor went back down to earth and found the prostitute.

'I'm sorry about last night,' he apologized. 'But you see, I'm Thor.'

'You're Thor?' shouted the girl, 'What about me? I can't even pith.'

Bad news for new father

A man is waiting nervously for news of his new-born baby when a nurse walks in. 'It's bad news,' she says. 'Your baby is badly deformed.'

Naturally the man tells himself that he will love the baby whatever it looks like. The midwife then leads the man out to the incubators. Passing a baby that is no more than a head, the midwife says 'Brace yourself, dear – your baby is a lot worse than this.'

Finally they arrive at the incubator and the father stares open-mouthed at his child. For there, sitting on the blanket, is a pair of eyeballs blinking away. 'I'm sorry,' offers the midwife.

The man, holding back tears, says, 'It's my baby and

I'll look after it the best I can.'

He gives the little eyes a tender wave.

'I wouldn't bother doing that,' says the midwife. 'It's blind.'

The DIY expert

A wife, frustrated by her husband's bone-idleness around the house, especially in the DIY department, sees cause for concern one day when the toilet clogs up. She decides to ask him if he'd mind seeing to it, and is greeted with a gruff, 'Who do I look like? A toilet cleaner?'

The next day the waste disposal unit seizes up. Summoning all her courage, she says, 'Sorry to bother you, dear. The waste disposal's broken – would you try to fix it for me?'

'Who do I look like? Some sort of plumber? Get me a beer and sod off!' is the reply.

To cap it all, the next day the washing machine

goes on the blink and, taking her life in her hands, the wife addresses the sofa-bound slob: 'Darling, I know you're busy, but the washing machine's packed up.'

'Oh, and I suppose I look like a bloody washing-machine man?' her old man says.

Finally fed up, she calls out three different repairmen to come and fix her appliances.

That evening, she informs her husband of this. He frowns angrily and asks, 'So how much will it cost?'

'Well, they said I could pay them either by baking a cake or having sex,' she says.

'What type of cakes did you bake?' he growls.

'Who do I look like? Delia Smith?'

Back to priest school

Father Patrick was talking to his replacement in a small village church.

'Father Michael,' he says, 'you'll be looking after my flock from now on.'

'But where do I start?' the young priest replies. 'You've been hearing confessions for over 50 years, I'll be lost.'

'Don't worry,' says Father Patrick, 'I've written a list of sins and absolutions on the wall in the confessional box. Look up the sin and it will tell you next to it what to say. After a while you'll get to know the congregation and you'll be okay.'

One week later, Father Michael is sitting in the

FHM

confessional box looking at his mentor's list when his first visitor arrives. 'Forgive me Father, for I have sinned,' says a female voice. 'I had to give my husband a gobble last night.'

The priest searches the wall but can't find the correct reply anywhere. In desperation he pulls open the curtain of the box and stops a choirboy.

'Oi! What did the old priest give for a gobble?'

'A Kit-Kat,' the lad replies.

The hygenic waiter

On being seated at a restaurant table, a gentleman becomes somewhat embarrassed when he knocks the spoon off with his elbow. A nearby waiter calmly picks it up and produces another shiny spoon from his pocket, which he places on the table.

Suitably impressed, the diner enquires, 'Do all waiters carry spare spoons on them?'

The waiter replies, 'Indeed, sir, it is in fact company policy, ever since our efficiency expert determined that 17.8 per cent of our clients knock the spoon off the table. By carrying a spare spoon on our person, we save on trips to the kitchen'

After the gentleman has finished his meal and paid the bill, he wanders over to the same waiter and says

FHM

to him, 'You will, of course, forgive me, but do you know you have a piece of string hanging from your fly?'

'Indeed, sir,' the waiter begins, 'Our efficiency expert determined that we were spending too much time washing our hands after going to the toilet. Thus, by attaching this piece of string to my penis I avoid touching myself: I go, and then I return to work. It saves a lot of time.'

'But how do you put it back in your trousers?' asks the curious diner.

'Well sir, I can't speak on behalf of my colleagues, but I just use the spoon.'

Clever lad

Little 10-year-old Freddie goes for a long weekend with his uncle, a wealthy Hampshire farm owner. One evening, as Uncle John and his wife are entertaining guests with cocktails, they are interrupted by an out-of-breath Freddie who shouts out, 'Uncle John! Come quick! The bull is fucking the cow!'

Uncle John, highly embarrassed, takes young Freddie aside, and explains that a certain amount of decorum is required. 'You should have said, "The bull is surprising the cow" – not some filth picked up in the playground,' he says.

A few days later, Freddie comes in again as his aunt and uncle are entertaining. 'Uncle John! The bull is

FHM

surprising the cows!'

The adults share a knowing grin. Uncle John says, 'Thank you, Freddie, but surely you meant to say the cow, not cows. A bull cannot "surprise" more than one cow at a time, you know ...'

'Yes, he can!' replies his obstinate nephew. 'He's fucking the horse!'

Whole lotta shaking going on

Alf and Mabel have been married for 60 years, and they live in a home for the old and infirm. One day Alf comes into their room and announces, 'Mabel, I know we've been together for 60 years, and we've been through a lot of hard times together, but I'm afraid I've got some bad news. I'm leaving you.'

'Why?' gasps the shocked old lady.

'I'm going out with Vera next door,' he replies.

'Vera? What does she do for you that I don't?'

'She gives me oral sex,' admits Alf.

'But ... but Alfred, I give you oral sex too,' exclaims Mabel.

'Maybe,' says Alf, 'but you don't have Parkinson's Disease.'

The power of suggestion

A blonde walks in to her local clinic and asks to see the doctor. When she's admitted, the doctor is a little perturbed to see she's wearing headphones and asks her to remove them.

'I'm afraid I can't or I'll die,' she replies.

'Don't be so ridiculous,' the doctor says, reaching across to snatch them out of her ears. Immediately the woman turns red and falls on the floor.

In the name of science the doctor puts the headphones in his ears.

'Breath in, breath out ...' says a soothing voice.

The power of photography

While enjoying a drink with his mate one night, Trevor decides to try his luck with an attractive lady sitting by the bar. She lets him join her for a drink and to his surprise asks him to accompany her home. They spend the night hard at it. Finally they finish; Trevor rolls off, pulls out a cigarette and looks for his lighter. He asks his new love if she has a light.

'There might be some matches in the top drawer,' she replies.

Opening the drawer he finds some matches on top of a framed photo of another man. Naturally he begins to worry.

'Is this your husband?' he enquires nervously.

'No, silly,' she replies.
'Your boyfriend then?'
'No,' she replies, snuggling up to him.
'Who is he, then?'
'That's me, before the operation.'

Declan the crab

Declan the humble crab and Katie the lobster princess were madly and passionately in love. For months they enjoyed an idyllic relationship, until one day Katie scuttled over to Declan in tears.

'We can't see each other anymore,' she sobbed.

'Why?' gasped Declan.

'Daddy says that crabs are too common,' she wailed. 'He says that no daughter of his will marry a creature that walks sideways.'

Declan was shattered, and walked away to drink himself in to oblivion.

That night, the great lobster ball was taking place. The lobster princess refused to join in the merriment.

Suddenly the doors opened and Declan the crab strode in. The dancing stopped, and all eyes were on Declan as he made his way over to Katie's father. All could see that he was walking forwards. Step by step he made his way over to the throne and looked the King Lobster in the eye. There was a deadly hush.

Finally, the crab spoke. 'Fuck, I'm pissed.'

Strength in numbers

Hacking his way through dense jungle, an explorer comes across a pygmy standing over a dead elephant.

'Did you kill this?' asked the explorer.

'Yes,' replied the tiny man.

'That's amazing! I've never seen such a thing. What did you use?'

'A club,' shrugged the pygmy.

'It must have been a bloody big club!'

'Indeed it was,' said the pygmy. 'There must have been about 300 of us.'

A disappointed father

Tommy ran home from school, as he couldn't wait to break his good news. 'Mum, Mum!' he yelled. 'I had sex with my geography teacher today!

Dad, Dad! Guess what, I had sex with my geography teacher.'

'I'm proud of you, son,' the father replied, to the mother's disbelief.

'I think now you're old enough to ride your brother's bike.'

Tommy's face dropped in disappointment.

'I can't. My arse hurts.'

Hard decision

A man goes to his doctor and admits that he has a sexual problem.

'I just can't get it up for my wife any more,' he says.

'Don't worry, Mr Williams,' says the doctor. 'Bring your wife in and I'll see what I can do.'

The couple come in the next day and the doctor asks the wife to remove her clothes. Then he asks her to turn around and jump up and down. He turns to the man.

'You're fine,' he says. 'She didn't give me an erection either.'

Genuine excuse

Pete rings his boss at work and says, 'Look, I'm really sorry, but I can't come to work today. I'm sick.'

'Sick!' screams his boss. 'Sick! This is the tenth time this month, Pete. Exactly how sick are you?'

'Well,' replies Pete. 'I'm in bed with my 12-year-old sister.'

A quiet drink spoiled

Three lads are enjoying a quiet night in a pub, when a fourth stumbles in and orders a beer. Spying the group, the drunk stumbles over, points at one of the boys and shouts: 'I've shagged your mum!'

The lads ignored him and returned to their pints. He shouts again: 'Up the arse!'

Although irritated, they ignore him again. The drunk stands up again points at the boy and yells: 'Your Mum's sucked my cock!'

The boy looks up wearily. 'You're drunk, Dad. Go home.'

FHM

Singer mishears crowd

Sir Cliff Richard is performing in Japan on the last leg of a successful world tour. The audience go wild as Cliff asks them if there is anything he can sing especially for them.

'Tits and fanny!' scream the audience.

'I can't sing that,' says Cliff. 'I'm a devout Christian.'

'Tits and fanny!' scream the crowd.

'Oh, come on,' says Cliff.

'Tits and fanny!' scream the crowd.

'Okay, okay,' says Cliff. 'But I don't know how it goes.'

'Tits and fanny ...' sing the crowd in unison. ' ... how we don't talk anymore.'

How the press works

Two boys are playing football in the park when one of them is attacked by a rottweiler. Thinking quickly, his friend rips a plank of wood from a nearby fence, forces it into the dog's collar and twists it, breaking the dog's neck.

All the while, a newspaper reporter who was taking a stroll through the park is watching. He rushes over, introduces himself and takes out his pad and pencil to start his story for the next edition. He writes, 'Manchester City fan saves friend from vicious animal.'

The boy interrupts: 'But I'm not a City fan.'

The reporter starts again: 'Manchester United fan rescues friend from horrific attack.'

The boy interrupts again: 'I'm not a United fan either.'

'Who do you support, then?'

'Liverpool,' replies the boy.

So the reporter starts again: 'Scouse bastard kills family pet.'

Playing through

Some friends were playing a round of golf when they heard shouts in the distance. Looking across, they watched amazed as a buxom lady ran onto the fairway, pulled off some of her clothes and sprinted off up the course. Not two minutes later, two men in white coats appeared and asked which way the woman had gone. They pointed up the course and the two men ran off in that direction.

Bemused, the golfers carried on with their game, but were again disturbed by another man. This time he was staggering over the hill, panting with the effort of carrying two buckets of sand. Between wheezes, the newcomer too asked which way the woman had gone, then tottered away. Increasingly baffled, the golf party ran after the figure. 'What the hell is going on?' they asked.

Gasping, the man explained: 'The lady has escaped from our treatment clinic. She has acute nymphomania, and as soon as she gets all her clothes off, the nearest man is ravished.'

'But why do you need two buckets of sand?' shouted the golfers after him.

'Well, I caught her the last time she escaped,' panted the man. 'This time, I needed a handicap.'

Three little words

An elderly gentleman shuffles into a newspaper office and asks if he can place a piece in the obituaries section.

'No problem sir,' says the young girl behind the desk. 'That'll be a pound per word.'

Nodding slowly, the old man writes 'Doris is dead' on a piece of paper, and forlornly passes it back to the girl.

'Is that all you want to put in it?' asks the girl.

The pensioner looks at her with sad eyes. 'I'm afraid I only have three pounds, my dear,' he says, and begins to shuffle out of the door.

The girl, feeling sorry for the old man, says she will

FHM

go up and speak to the editor. 'Wait – I'll see if we can work something out.'

Moments later, she returns from the office, grinning broadly. 'Good news,' she says. 'The editor says you can have another three pounds worth of words.'

Smiling gratefully, the old man takes another piece of paper and thinks for moment. Shakily, he then writes: 'Doris Is Dead. Metro For Sale'.

Patient takes advice too far

After suffering from severe headaches for years with no relief, Trevor is referred to a headache specialist by his family GP.

'The trouble is,' Trevor tells the specialist, 'I get this blinding pain, like a knife across my scalp and ...'

He is interrupted by the doctor, 'And a heavy throbbing right behind the left ear?'

'Yes! Exactly! How did you know?'

'Well, I myself suffered from that same type of headache for many years. It is caused by a tension in the scalp muscles. This is how I cured it: every day I would give my wife oral sex.'

'Is that all it takes?' says Trevor, intrigued.

'Oh no,' says the doctor. 'When she came she would squeeze her legs together with all her strength and the pressure would relieve the tension in my head. Try that every day for two weeks and come back and let me know how it goes.'

Two weeks go by and Trevor returns, grinning. 'Doc, I'm a new man! I haven't had a headache since I started this treatment! I can't thank you enough.'

'That's fine,' says the doctor. 'I was glad to pass on a personal cure.'

'By the way,' says Trevor, standing up to leave. 'You have a lovely home.'

The best ferret in the world

A man is having a quiet drink in a pub when a tramp comes up and asks, 'Wanna buy this for £50?' He pulls a ferret from his pocket.

'What the hell would I want to buy that for?' asks the man.

'This ferret will give you the best blow job of your life,' the tramp says.

The guy thinks his leg is being pulled, and tells the tramp to sling his hook. Undeterred, the tramps continues, 'Look, if you don't believe me, take it outside for a free trial.'

The guy takes the ferret out to the back of the pub. Straight away, the animal unzips his trousers and

FHM

gives him the best blow job of his life. So the guy carries the ferret back into the pub, gives the tramp £50 and takes the animal home.

When his battleaxe of a wife opens the front door, the man proudly holds up the ferret.

'Look what I've bought for £50,' he proclaims.

'What on earth did you buy that for?' she asks angrily.

'This ferret gave me the best blow job of my life!' he exclaims.

'Well,' she says, annoyed. 'What the hell do you want me to do with it?'

The man replies, 'Teach it how to cook – and then fuck off!'

Tall order

A milkman is making his deliveries and finds a note attached to a customer's door saying, 'I need 45 gallons of milk.'

He knocks at the door and a beautiful, dumb blonde answers it.

'Is this a mistake?' the milkman asks.

'No,' she says. 'I was watching a talk-show and it said bathing in milk is a good aphrodisiac.'

'Really?' replies the milkman. 'Do you want that pasteurized?'

'No, up to my tits will be fine,' she says.

Caught short

Two dwarfs have just won the lottery, so they go out and hire two prostitutes and two hotel rooms. The first dwarf tries desperately all night to get an erection, but all he can hear from the next room is, 'One, two, three, huh!' This goes on all night.

The next morning, the second dwarf asks, 'So, how did it go?'

The first dwarf replies, 'Shit, I couldn't get an erection. How was your night?'

The second dwarf turns round and replies, 'Even worse, I couldn't even get on the bed.'

It always comes in higher ...

The police have just arrested Fred West. They take him down to the cells and start to interrogate him. They say, 'Right then, you bastard, how many have you killed?'

Fred says, '17.'

So the coppers spend weeks digging up his house - and find 25 bodies. They go back to Fred and say, 'You bastard, you told us you killed 17.'

And Fred says, 'Yeah, but I'm a builder. It was only an estimate.'